MznLnx

Missing Links Exam Preps

Exam Prep for

Management for Engineers, Scientists and Technologists

Chelsom, Payne & Reavill, 2nd Edition

The MznLnx Exam Prep is your link from the texbook and lecture to your exams.
The MznLnx Exam Preps are unauthorized and comprehensive reviews of your textbooks.

All material provided by MznLnx and Rico Publications (c) 2010
Textbook publishers and textbook authors do not particpate in or contribute to these reviews.

MznLnx

Rico
Publications

Exam Prep for Management for Engineers, Scientists and Technologists
2nd Edition
Chelsom, Payne & Reavill

Publisher: Raymond Houge
Assistant Editor: Michael Rouger
Text and Cover Designer: Lisa Buckner
Marketing Manager: Sara Swagger
Project Manager, Editorial Production: Jerry Emerson
Art Director: Vernon Lowerui

Product Manager: Dave Mason
Editorial Assitant: Rachel Guzmanji
Pedagogy: Debra Long
Cover Image: Jim Reed/Getty Images
Text and Cover Printer: City Printing, Inc.
Compositor: Media Mix, Inc.

(c) 2010 Rico Publications

ALL RIGHTS RESERVED. No part of this work covered by the copyright may be reproduced or used in any form or by an means--graphic, electronic, or mechanical, including photocopying, recording, taping, Web distribution, information storage, and retrieval systems, or in any other manner--without the written permission of the publisher.

Printed in the United States
ISBN:

For more information about our products, contact us at:
Dave.Mason@RicoPublications.com

For permission to use material from this text or product, submit a request online to:
Dave.Mason@RicoPublications.com

Contents

CHAPTER 1
Business basics — 1

CHAPTER 2
The business environment — 3

CHAPTER 3
Management styles: From Taylorism to McKinsey`s 7Ss — 4

CHAPTER 4
Management of quality — 5

CHAPTER 5
Materials management — 8

CHAPTER 6
Managing design and new product development — 9

CHAPTER 7
Organizations — 10

CHAPTER 8
Managing to succeed — 12

CHAPTER 9
Human resource management—the individual — 14

CHAPTER 10
Groups of people — 17

CHAPTER 11
Communication — 23

CHAPTER 12
Work study — 25

CHAPTER 13
Costing and pricing — 27

CHAPTER 14
Measuring financial performance — 32

CHAPTER 15
Project investment decisions — 41

CHAPTER 16
Maintenance management — 44

CHAPTER 17
Project management — 46

CHAPTER 18
Networks for projects — 52

CHAPTER 19
Project management — managing construction procurement — 53

CHAPTER 20
Inventory management — 56

Contents (Cont.)

CHAPTER 21
   Management of the supply system   58
CHAPTER 22
   Marketing   62
CHAPTER 23
   A case study in starting an SME   67
ANSWER KEY   69

TO THE STUDENT

COMPREHENSIVE

The *MznLnx* Exam Prep series is designed to help you pass your exams. Editors at MznLnx review your textbooks and then prepare these practice exams to help you master the textbook material. Unlike study guides, workbooks, and practice tests provided by the texbook publisher and textbook authors, *MznLnx* gives you **all** of the material in each chapter in exam form, not just samples, so you can be sure to nail your exam.

MECHANICAL

The MznLnx Exam Prep series creates exams that will help you learn the subject matter as well as test you on your understanding. Each question is designed to help you master the concept. Just working through the exams, you gain an understanding of the subject--its a simple mechanical process that produces success.

INTEGRATED STUDY GUIDE AND REVIEW

MznLnx is not just a set of exams designed to test you, its also a comprehensive review of the subject content. Each exam question is also a review of the concept, making sure that you will get the answer correct without having to go to other sources of material. You learn as you go! Its the easiest way to pass an exam.

HUMOR

Studying can be tedious and dry. MznLnx's instructional design includes moderate humor within the exam questions on occassion, to break the tedium and revitalize the brain

Chapter 1. Business basics

1. A _____ is a list of the general tasks and responsibilities of a position. Typically, it also includes to whom the position reports, specifications such as the qualifications needed by the person in the job, salary range for the position, etc. A _____ is usually developed by conducting a job analysis, which includes examining the tasks and sequences of tasks necessary to perform the job.

    a. Recruitment Process Insourcing
    b. Recruitment advertising
    c. Job description
    d. Recruitment

2. _____ refers to the movement of cash into or out of a business or financial product. It is usually measured during a specified, finite period of time. Measurement of _____ can be used

    - to determine a project's rate of return or value. The time of _____s into and out of projects are used as inputs in financial models such as internal rate of return, and net present value.
    - to determine problems with a business's liquidity. Being profitable does not necessarily mean being liquid. A company can fail because of a shortage of cash, even while profitable.
    - as an alternate measure of a business's profits when it is believed that accrual accounting concepts do not represent economic realities. For example, a company may be notionally profitable but generating little operational cash (as may be the case for a company that barters its products rather than selling for cash.) In such a case, the company may be deriving additional operating cash by issuing shares evaluating default risk, re-investment requirements, etc.

    _____ is a generic term used differently depending on the context. It may be defined by users for their own purposes.

    a. Gross profit
    b. Cash flow
    c. Gross profit margin
    d. Sweat equity

3. _____ is used in finance as a measure of the returns that a company is realising from its capital employed. It is commonly used as a measure for comparing the performance between businesses and for assessing whether a business generates enough returns to pay for its cost of capital.

    Net Profit / Capital Employed X 100

    _____ compares earnings with capital invested in the company.

    a. Return on Capital Employed
    b. Return on equity
    c. Times interest earned
    d. Financial ratio

Chapter 1. Business basics

4. _____ is a work methodology based on the parallelization of tasks (ie. concurrently.) It refers to an approach used in product development in which functions of design engineering, manufacturing engineering and other functions are integrated to reduce the elapsed time required to bring a new product to the market.

   a. Concurrent engineering
   b. Work package
   c. Project management
   d. Critical Chain Project Management

5. _____ is the process whereby an organization establishes the parameters within which programs, investments, and acquisitions are reaching the desired results. Performance Reference Model of the Federal Enterprise Architecture, 2005.

This process of measuring performance often requires the use of statistical evidence to determine progress toward specific defined organizational objectives.

There are many types of measurements.

   a. Performance measurement
   b. Crisis management
   c. Workflow
   d. CIFMS

6. The doctrine of _____ in contract law provides that a contract cannot confer rights or impose obligations arising under it on any person or agent except the parties to it.

The premise is that only parties to contracts should be able to sue to enforce their rights or claim damages as such. However, the doctrine has proven problematic due to its implications upon contracts made for the benefit of third parties who are unable to enforce the obligations of the contracting parties.

   a. Privity
   b. Privacy Act of 1974
   c. Blue sky law
   d. Comprehensive Environmental Response, Compensation, and Liability Act

Chapter 2. The business environment

1. A _____ is the system of organizations, people, technology, activities, information and resources involved in moving a product or service from supplier to customer. _____ activities transform natural resources, raw materials and components into a finished product that is delivered to the end customer. In sophisticated _____ systems, used products may re-enter the _____ at any point where residual value is recyclable.
    a. Wholesalers
    b. Packaging
    c. Drop shipping
    d. Supply chain

2. _____ is a strategic planning method used to evaluate the Strengths, Weaknesses, Opportunities, and Threats involved in a project or in a business venture. It involves specifying the objective of the business venture or project and identifying the internal and external factors that are favorable and unfavorable to achieving that objective. The technique is credited to Albert Humphrey, who led a convention at Stanford University in the 1960s and 1970s using data from Fortune 500 companies.
    a. Corporate image
    b. Market share
    c. Marketing
    d. SWOT analysis

3. In finance, the _____s between two currencies specifies how much one currency is worth in terms of the other. It is the value of a foreign nation's currency in terms of the home nation's currency. For example an _____ of 102 Japanese yen to the United States dollar means that JPY 102 is worth the same as USD 1.
    a. Exchange rate
    b. A4e
    c. A Stake in the Outcome
    d. AAAI

4. _____ is the statistical study of all populations. It can be a very general science that can be applied to any kind of dynamic population, that is, one that changes over time or space It encompasses the study of the size, structure and distribution of populations, and spatial and/or temporal changes in them in response to birth, migration, aging and death.
    a. 33 Strategies of War
    b. 1990 Clean Air Act
    c. Demography
    d. 28-hour day

Chapter 3. Management styles: From Taylorism to McKinsey`s 7Ss

1. _____, widely known as F. W. Taylor, was an American mechanical engineer who sought to improve industrial efficiency. He is regarded as the father of scientific management, and was one of the first management consultants.

Taylor was one of the intellectual leaders of the Efficiency Movement and his ideas, broadly conceived, were highly influential in the Progressive Era.

   a. Jonah Jacob Goldberg
   b. Geoffrey Colvin
   c. Douglas N. Daft
   d. Frederick Winslow Taylor

2. In economics, business, retail, and accounting, a _____ is the value of money that has been used up to produce something, and hence is not available for use anymore. In economics, a _____ is an alternative that is given up as a result of a decision. In business, the _____ may be one of acquisition, in which case the amount of money expended to acquire it is counted as _____.
   a. Cost allocation
   b. Fixed costs
   c. Cost overrun
   d. Cost

3. _____ is an integrated communications-based process through which individuals and communities discover that existing and newly-identified needs and wants may be satisfied by the products and services of others.

_____ is defined by the American _____ Association as the activity, set of institutions, and processes for creating, communicating, delivering, and exchanging offerings that have value for customers, clients, partners, and society at large. The term developed from the original meaning which referred literally to going to market, as in shopping, or going to a market to buy or sell goods or services.

   a. Disruptive technology
   b. Market development
   c. Customer relationship management
   d. Marketing

Chapter 4. Management of quality

1. In economics, business, retail, and accounting, a _____ is the value of money that has been used up to produce something, and hence is not available for use anymore. In economics, a _____ is an alternative that is given up as a result of a decision. In business, the _____ may be one of acquisition, in which case the amount of money expended to acquire it is counted as _____.
   a. Cost overrun
   b. Cost allocation
   c. Fixed costs
   d. Cost

2. The concept of quality costs is a means to quantify the total _____-related efforts and deficiencies. It was first described by Armand V. Feigenbaum in a 1956 Harvard Business Review article.

   Prior to its introduction, the general perception was that higher quality requires higher costs, either by buying better materials or machines or by hiring more labor.

   a. Cost accounting
   b. Fixed costs
   c. Quality costs
   d. Cost of quality

3. A _____ is a research instrument consisting of a series of questions and other prompts for the purpose of gathering information from respondents. Although they are often designed for statistical analysis of the responses, this is not always the case. The _____ was invented by Sir Francis Galton.
   a. Questionnaire construction
   b. Structured interview
   c. Questionnaire
   d. Mystery shoppers

4. _____ is one of the managerial functions like planning, organizing, staffing and directing. It is an important function because it helps to check the errors and to take the corrective action so that deviation from standards are minimized and stated goals of the organization are achieved in desired manner. According to modern concepts, _____ is a foreseeing action whereas earlier concept of _____ was used only when errors were detected. _____ in management means setting standards, measuring actual performance and taking corrective action.
   a. Decision tree pruning
   b. Turnover
   c. Control
   d. Schedule of reinforcement

Chapter 4. Management of quality

5. The _____ in statistical process control is a tool used to determine whether a manufacturing or business process is in a state of statistical control or not.

If the chart indicates that the process is currently under control then it can be used with confidence to predict the future performance of the process. If the chart indicates that the process being monitored is not in control, the pattern it reveals can help determine the source of variation to be eliminated to bring the process back into control.

   a. Simple moving average
   b. Failure rate
   c. Time series analysis
   d. Control chart

6. _____ is the management of the flow of goods, information and other resources, including energy and people, between the point of origin and the point of consumption in order to meet the requirements of consumers (frequently, and originally, military organizations.) _____ involves the integration of information, transportation, inventory, warehousing, material-handling, and packaging, and occasionally security. _____ is a channel of the supply chain which adds the value of time and place utility.
   a. Logistics
   b. Third-party logistics
   c. 28-hour day
   d. 1990 Clean Air Act

7. _____ is a business management strategy aimed at embedding awareness of quality in all organizational processes. _____ has been widely used in manufacturing, education, hospitals, call centers, government, and service industries, as well as NASA space and science programs.

As defined by the International Organization for Standardization (ISO):

> '_____ is a management approach for an organization, centered on quality, based on the participation of all its members and aiming at long-term success through customer satisfaction, and benefits to all members of the organization and to society.' ISO 8402:1994

One major aim is to reduce variation from every process so that greater consistency of effort is obtained. (Royse, D., Thyer, B., Padgett D., ' Logan T., 2006)

a. Quality management
b. 28-hour day
c. 1990 Clean Air Act
d. Total quality management

8. _____ is a work methodology based on the parallelization of tasks (ie. concurrently.) It refers to an approach used in product development in which functions of design engineering, manufacturing engineering and other functions are integrated to reduce the elapsed time required to bring a new product to the market.

a. Project management
b. Work package
c. Critical Chain Project Management
d. Concurrent engineering

9. _____ is a family of standards for quality management systems. _____ is maintained by ISO, the International Organization for Standardization and is administered by accreditation and certification bodies. The rules are updated, the time and changes in the requirements for quality, motivate change.

a. A4e
b. A Stake in the Outcome
c. AAAI
d. ISO 9000

10. _____ is a business management strategy, initially implemented by Motorola, that today enjoys widespread application in many sectors of industry.

_____ seeks to improve the quality of process outputs by identifying and removing the causes of defects (errors) and variation in manufacturing and business processes. It uses a set of quality management methods, including statistical methods, and creates a special infrastructure of people within the organization ('Black Belts' etc.)

a. Production line
b. Six Sigma
c. Takt time
d. Theory of constraints

Chapter 5. Materials management

1. _____ is used in finance as a measure of the returns that a company is realising from its capital employed. It is commonly used as a measure for comparing the performance between businesses and for assessing whether a business generates enough returns to pay for its cost of capital.

Net Profit / Capital Employed X 100

_____ compares earnings with capital invested in the company.

   a. Financial ratio
   b. Return on equity
   c. Return on Capital Employed
   d. Times interest earned

2. _____ is the branch of logistics that deals with the tangible components of a supply chain. Specifically, this covers the acquisition of spare parts and replacements, quality control of purchasing and ordering such parts, and the standards involved in ordering, shipping, and warehousing the said parts.

A large component of _____ is ensuring that parts and materials used in the supply chain meet minimum requirements by performing quality assurance (QA.)

   a. Vendor Managed Inventory
   b. Supply-Chain Operations Reference
   c. Delayed differentiation
   d. Materials management

Chapter 6. Managing design and new product development

1. _____ or net present worth (NPW) is defined as the total present value (PV) of a time series of cash flows. It is a standard method for using the time value of money to appraise long-term projects. Used for capital budgeting, and widely throughout economics, it measures the excess or shortfall of cash flows, in present value terms, once financing charges are met.
   a. 1990 Clean Air Act
   b. Discounted cash flow
   c. Present value
   d. Net present value

2. _____ is the value on a given date of a future payment or series of future payments, discounted to reflect the time value of money and other factors such as investment risk. _____ calculations are widely used in business and economics to provide a means to compare cash flows at different times on a meaningful 'like to like' basis.

   If offered a choice between $100 today or $100 in one year, everyone will choose $100 today.

   a. Net present value
   b. Present value
   c. 1990 Clean Air Act
   d. Discounted cash flow

3. _____ is a work methodology based on the parallelization of tasks (ie. concurrently.) It refers to an approach used in product development in which functions of design engineering, manufacturing engineering and other functions are integrated to reduce the elapsed time required to bring a new product to the market.
   a. Project management
   b. Work package
   c. Critical Chain Project Management
   d. Concurrent engineering

4. A _____ is the system of organizations, people, technology, activities, information and resources involved in moving a product or service from supplier to customer. _____ activities transform natural resources, raw materials and components into a finished product that is delivered to the end customer. In sophisticated _____ systems, used products may re-enter the _____ at any point where residual value is recyclable.
   a. Supply chain
   b. Drop shipping
   c. Wholesalers
   d. Packaging

Chapter 7. Organizations

1. A _____ is typically described as a deliberate plan of action to guide decisions and achieve rational outcome(s.) However, the term may also be used to denote what is actually done, even though it is unplanned.

The term may apply to government, private sector organizations and groups, and individuals.

   a. 33 Strategies of War
   b. 28-hour day
   c. 1990 Clean Air Act
   d. Policy

2. _____ refers to the process of screening, and selecting qualified people for a job at an organization or firm mid- and large-size organizations and companies often retain professional recruiters or outsource some of the process to _____ agencies. External _____ is the process of attracting and selecting employees from outside the organization.

The _____ industry has four main types of agencies: employment agencies, _____ websites and job search engines, 'headhunters' for executive and professional _____, and in-house _____.

   a. Referral recruitment
   b. Labour hire
   c. Recruitment Process Outsourcing
   d. Recruitment

3. _____ is a type of organizational management in which people with similar skills are pooled for work assignments. For example, all engineers may be in one engineering department and report to an engineering manager, but these same engineers may be assigned to different projects and report to a project manager while working on that project. Therefore, each engineer may have to work under several managers to get their job done.
   a. Span of control
   b. Central Administration
   c. Management development
   d. Matrix management

4. _____ is a term in management and corporate restructuring that refers to a planned reduction in the number of layers of a management hierarchy.
   a. Product innovation
   b. Delayering
   c. Mass market
   d. Supervisory board

5. _____ refers to increasing the spiritual, political, social or economic strength of individuals and communities. It often involves the empowered developing confidence in their own capacities.

The term Human _____ covers a vast landscape of meanings, interpretations, definitions and disciplines ranging from psychology and philosophy to the highly commercialized Self-Help industry and Motivational sciences.

a. Empowerment
b. AAAI
c. A Stake in the Outcome
d. A4e

Chapter 8. Managing to succeed

1. _____ is the process of comparing the cost, cycle time, productivity, or quality of a specific process or method to another that is widely considered to be an industry standard or best practice. Essentially, _____ provides a snapshot of the performance of your business and helps you understand where you are in relation to a particular standard. The result is often a business case for making changes in order to make improvements.

   a. Complementors
   b. Cost leadership
   c. Competitive heterogeneity
   d. Benchmarking

2. _____ has been described as the 'process of social influence in which one person can enlist the aid and support of others in the accomplishment of a common task' . A definition more inclusive of followers comes from Alan Keith of Genentech who said '_____ is ultimately about creating a way for people to contribute to making something extraordinary happen.'

   _____ is one of the most salient aspects of the organizational context. However, defining _____ has been challenging.

   a. 28-hour day
   b. Situational leadership
   c. 1990 Clean Air Act
   d. Leadership

3. _____ are job factors that can cause dissatisfaction if missing but do not necessarily motivate employees if increased.

   _____ have mostly to do with the job environment. These factors are important or notable only when they are lacking.

   a. Split shift
   b. Work-at-home scheme
   c. Hygiene factors
   d. Work system

4. In finance, the _____s between two currencies specifies how much one currency is worth in terms of the other. It is the value of a foreign nation's currency in terms of the home nation's currency. For example an _____ of 102 Japanese yen to the United States dollar means that JPY 102 is worth the same as USD 1.

a. AAAI
b. A4e
c. A Stake in the Outcome
d. Exchange rate

Chapter 9. Human resource management—the individual

1. The doctrine of _____ in contract law provides that a contract cannot confer rights or impose obligations arising under it on any person or agent except the parties to it.

The premise is that only parties to contracts should be able to sue to enforce their rights or claim damages as such. However, the doctrine has proven problematic due to its implications upon contracts made for the benefit of third parties who are unable to enforce the obligations of the contracting parties.

   a. Blue sky law
   b. Privity
   c. Privacy Act of 1974
   d. Comprehensive Environmental Response, Compensation, and Liability Act

2. In psychology, _____ reflects a person's overall evaluation or appraisal of his or her own worth.

_____ encompasses beliefs (for example, 'I am competent/incompetent') and emotions (for example, triumph/despair, pride/shame.) Behavior may reflect _____

   a. 33 Strategies of War
   b. Self-esteem
   c. 28-hour day
   d. 1990 Clean Air Act

3. A _____ is a research instrument consisting of a series of questions and other prompts for the purpose of gathering information from respondents. Although they are often designed for statistical analysis of the responses, this is not always the case. The _____ was invented by Sir Francis Galton.

   a. Questionnaire
   b. Mystery shoppers
   c. Structured interview
   d. Questionnaire construction

4. _____ was developed by Frederick Herzberg, a psychologist who found that job satisfaction and job dissatisfaction acted independently of each other. _____ states that there are certain factors in the workplace that cause job satisfaction, while a separate set of factors cause dissatisfaction.

   a. 1990 Clean Air Act
   b. Need for Achievement
   c. Need for power
   d. Two-factor theory

Chapter 9. Human resource management—the individual

5. _____ involves establishing specific, measurable and time-targeted objectives. Work on the theory of goal-setting suggests that it's an effective tool for making progress by ensuring that participants in a group with a common goal are clearly aware of what is expected from them if an objective is to be achieved. On a personal level, setting goals is a process that allows people to specify then work towards their own objectives - most commonly with financial or career-based goals.
    a. Goal setting
    b. Catfish effect
    c. Resource-based view
    d. Digital strategy

6. _____ attempts to explain relational satisfaction in terms of perceptions of fair/unfair distributions of resources within interpersonal relationships. _____ is considered as one of the justice theories, It was first developed in 1962 by John Stacey Adams, a workplace and behavioral psychologist, who asserted that employees seek to maintain equity between the inputs that they bring to a job and the outcomes that they receive from it against the perceived inputs and outcomes of others (Adams, 1965.) The belief is that people value fair treatment which causes them to be motivated to keep the fairness maintained within the relationships of their co-workers and the organization.
    a. Equity theory
    b. A Stake in the Outcome
    c. AAAI
    d. A4e

7. _____ is about the mental processes regarding choice, or choosing. It explains the processes that an individual undergoes to make choices. In organizational behavior study, _____ is a motivation theory first proposed by Victor Vroom of the Yale School of Management.
    a. A4e
    b. AAAI
    c. Expectancy theory
    d. A Stake in the Outcome

8. _____ is an attempt to motivate employees by giving them the opportunity to use the range of their abilities. It is an idea that was developed by the American psychologist Frederick Herzberg in the 1950s. It can be contrasted to job enlargement which simply increases the number of tasks without changing the challenge.
    a. Catfish effect
    b. Job enrichment
    c. Cash cow
    d. C-A-K-E

Chapter 9. Human resource management—the individual

9. In operant conditioning, _____ occurs when an event following a response causes an increase in the probability of that response occurring in the future. Response strength can be assessed by measures such as the frequency with which the response is made (for example, a pigeon may peck a key more times in the session), or the speed with which it is made (for example, a rat may run a maze faster.) The environment change contingent upon the response is called a reinforcer.

  a. Meetings, Incentives, Conferences, and Exhibitions
  b. Historiometry
  c. Diminishing Manufacturing Sources and Material Shortages
  d. Reinforcement

Chapter 10. Groups of people

1. _____ is a civil designation for persons who are incorporated in a fixed or permanent way to a society or group: regular member of the working staff, permanent staff distinguished from a supernumerary.

The term '_____' and its counterpart, 'supernumerary,' originated in Spanish and Latin American academy and government; it is now also used in countries all over the world, such as France, the U.S., England, Italy, etc.

There are _____ members of surgical organizations, of universities, of gastronomical associations, etc.

  a. Abraham Harold Maslow
  b. Adam Smith
  c. Affiliation
  d. Numerary

2. The goal of most research on _____ is to learn why and how small groups change over time. To do this, researchers examine patterns of change and continuity in groups over time. Aspects of a group that might be studied include the quality of the output produced by a group, the type and frequency of its activities, its cohesiveness, the existence of conflict, etc.
  a. 1990 Clean Air Act
  b. 28-hour day
  c. 33 Strategies of War
  d. Group development

3. A _____ is a list of the general tasks and responsibilities of a position. Typically, it also includes to whom the position reports, specifications such as the qualifications needed by the person in the job, salary range for the position, etc. A _____ is usually developed by conducting a job analysis, which includes examining the tasks and sequences of tasks necessary to perform the job.
  a. Recruitment Process Insourcing
  b. Recruitment advertising
  c. Recruitment
  d. Job description

4. _____ is a concept or doctrine, according to which individuals are to be held responsible for other people's actions by tolerating, ignoring without actively collaborating in these actions.

This concept is found in the Old Testament (or Tanakh), some examples include the account of the Flood, the Tower of Babel, Sodom and Gomorrah and in some interpretations, the Book of Joshua's Achan. In those records entire communities were punished on the act of the vast majority of their members, however it is impossible that there weren't any innocent people, or children too young to be responsible for their deeds.

Chapter 10. Groups of people

   a. Self-determination
   b. 1990 Clean Air Act
   c. 28-hour day
   d. Collective responsibility

5. _____ has been described as the 'process of social influence in which one person can enlist the aid and support of others in the accomplishment of a common task'. A definition more inclusive of followers comes from Alan Keith of Genentech who said '_____ is ultimately about creating a way for people to contribute to making something extraordinary happen.'

_____ is one of the most salient aspects of the organizational context. However, defining _____ has been challenging.

   a. Leadership
   b. 1990 Clean Air Act
   c. Situational leadership
   d. 28-hour day

6. The _____ is a concept from business management that was first described and popularized by Michael Porter in his 1985 best-seller, Competitive Advantage: Creating and Sustaining Superior Performance.

A _____ is a chain of activities. Products pass through all activities of the chain in order and at each activity the product gains some value. The chain of activities gives the products more added value than the sum of added values of all activities. It is important not to mix the concept of the _____ with the costs occurring throughout the activities.

   a. Mass marketing
   b. Value chain
   c. Market development
   d. Customer relationship management

7. _____ is a term that is used to describe a specialized form of management that is required to successfully lead engineering personnel and projects. The average Engineering Manager retires at 50-60 years of age. The term can be used to describe either functional management or project management- leading technical professionals who are working in the fields of product development, manufacturing, construction, design engineering, industrial engineering, technology, production, or any other field that employs personnel who perform an engineering function.

Chapter 10. Groups of people

a. Efficient Consumer Response
b. Executive development
c. ISO/TC 223
d. Engineering management

8. _____ refers to the movement of cash into or out of a business or financial product. It is usually measured during a specified, finite period of time. Measurement of _____ can be used

- to determine a project's rate of return or value. The time of _____s into and out of projects are used as inputs in financial models such as internal rate of return, and net present value.
- to determine problems with a business's liquidity. Being profitable does not necessarily mean being liquid. A company can fail because of a shortage of cash, even while profitable.
- as an alternate measure of a business's profits when it is believed that accrual accounting concepts do not represent economic realities. For example, a company may be notionally profitable but generating little operational cash (as may be the case for a company that barters its products rather than selling for cash.) In such a case, the company may be deriving additional operating cash by issuing shares evaluating default risk, re-investment requirements, etc.

_____ is a generic term used differently depending on the context. It may be defined by users for their own purposes.

a. Sweat equity
b. Gross profit
c. Gross profit margin
d. Cash flow

9. _____ of the learning curve effect and the closely related experience curve effect express the relationship between equations for experience and efficiency or between efficiency gains and investment in the effort. The experience of 'learning curves' was first observed by the 19th Century German psychologist Hermann Ebbinghaus according to the difficulty of memorizing varying numbers of verbal stimuli, and subsequent learning about the complex processes of learning are discussed in the

.

The rule used for representing the learning curve effect states that the more times a task has been performed, the less time will be required on each subsequent iteration.

a. Spatial Decision Support Systems
b. Distribution
c. Point biserial correlation coefficient
d. Models

Chapter 10. Groups of people

10. In finance, the _____ approach describes a method of valuing a project, company, or asset using the concepts of the time value of money. All future cash flows are estimated and discounted to give their present values. The discount rate used is generally the appropriate WACC, that reflects the risk of the cashflows.
   a. 1990 Clean Air Act
   b. Net present value
   c. Discounted cash flow
   d. Present value

11. _____ or specialization is the specialization of cooperative labour in specific, circumscribed tasks and roles, intended to increase the productivity of labour. Historically the growth of a more and more complex _____ is closely associated with the growth of total output and trade, the rise of capitalism, and of the complexity of industrialization processes. Later, the _____ reached the level of a scientifically-based management practice with the time and motion studies associated with Taylorism.
   a. Division of labour
   b. Labor force
   c. Departmentalization
   d. PATCOB

12. _____ is an advertisement in which a particular product specifically mentions a competitor by name for the express purpose of showing why the competitor is inferior to the product naming it.

This should not be confused with parody advertisements, where a fictional product is being advertised for the purpose of poking fun at the particular advertisement, nor should it be confused with the use of a coined brand name for the purpose of comparing the product without actually naming an actual competitor. ('Wikipedia tastes better and is less filling than the Encyclopedia Galactica.')

In the 1980s, during what has been referred to as the cola wars, soft-drink manufacturer Pepsi ran a series of advertisements where people, caught on hidden camera, in a blind taste test, chose Pepsi over rival Coca-Cola.

   a. 33 Strategies of War
   b. Comparative advertising
   c. 28-hour day
   d. 1990 Clean Air Act

13. _____ is the process of estimation in unknown situations. Prediction is a similar, but more general term. Both can refer to estimation of time series, cross-sectional or longitudinal data.

Chapter 10. Groups of people

a. 28-hour day
b. 33 Strategies of War
c. Forecasting
d. 1990 Clean Air Act

14. _____ refers to the process of screening, and selecting qualified people for a job at an organization or firm mid- and large-size organizations and companies often retain professional recruiters or outsource some of the process to _____ agencies. External _____ is the process of attracting and selecting employees from outside the organization.

The _____ industry has four main types of agencies: employment agencies, _____ websites and job search engines, 'headhunters' for executive and professional _____, and in-house _____.

a. Recruitment Process Outsourcing
b. Labour hire
c. Recruitment
d. Referral recruitment

15. _____ is a method by which the job performance of an employee is evaluated _____ is a part of career development.

_____s are regular reviews of employee performance within organizations

Generally, the aims of a _____ are to:

- Give feedback on performance to employees.
- Identify employee training needs.
- Document criteria used to allocate organizational rewards.
- Form a basis for personnel decisions: salary increases, promotions, disciplinary actions, etc.
- Provide the opportunity for organizational diagnosis and development.
- Facilitate communication between employee and administraton
- Validate selection techniques and human resource policies to meet federal Equal Employment Opportunity requirements.

A common approach to assessing performance is to use a numerical or scalar rating system whereby managers are asked to score an individual against a number of objectives/attributes. In some companies, employees receive assessments from their manager, peers, subordinates and customers while also performing a self assessment.

a. Progressive discipline
b. Human resource management
c. Personnel management
d. Performance appraisal

16. _____ is pay or salary, typically a monetary payment for services rendered, as in an employment. Usage of the word is considered formal.

_____ can include:

- Commission
- Compensation methods (in online advertising and internet marketing)
- Compensation
    - Executive compensation
    - Deferred compensation
- Employee stock option
- Fringe benefit
- Salary
- Wage

a. 33 Strategies of War
b. 1990 Clean Air Act
c. 28-hour day
d. Remuneration

Chapter 11. Communication

1. _____ describes the situation when output from (or information about the result of) an event or phenomenon in the past will influence the same event/phenomenon in the present or future. When an event is part of a chain of cause-and-effect that forms a circuit or loop, then the event is said to 'feed back' into itself.

_____ is also a synonym for:

- _____ signal; the information about the initial event that is the basis for subsequent modification of the event.
- _____ loop; the causal path that leads from the initial generation of the _____ signal to the subsequent modification of the event.

_____ is a mechanism, process or signal that is looped back to control a system within itself. Such a loop is called a _____ loop.

 a. Positive feedback
 b. 1990 Clean Air Act
 c. Feedback
 d. Feedback loop

2. The _____ refers to a cognitive bias whereby the perception of a particular trait is influenced by the perception of the former traits in a sequence of interpretations.

Edward L. Thorndike was the first to support the _____ with empirical research. In a psychology study published in 1920, Thorndike asked commanding officers to rate their soldiers; Thorndike found high cross-correlation between all positive and all negative traits.

 a. Cognitive biases
 b. Distinction bias
 c. Sunk costs
 d. Halo effect

3. _____ refers to the process of screening, and selecting qualified people for a job at an organization or firm mid- and large-size organizations and companies often retain professional recruiters or outsource some of the process to _____ agencies. External _____ is the process of attracting and selecting employees from outside the organization.

The _____ industry has four main types of agencies: employment agencies, _____ websites and job search engines, 'headhunters' for executive and professional _____, and in-house _____.

a. Referral recruitment
b. Labour hire
c. Recruitment Process Outsourcing
d. Recruitment

4. The doctrine of _____ in contract law provides that a contract cannot confer rights or impose obligations arising under it on any person or agent except the parties to it.

The premise is that only parties to contracts should be able to sue to enforce their rights or claim damages as such. However, the doctrine has proven problematic due to its implications upon contracts made for the benefit of third parties who are unable to enforce the obligations of the contracting parties.

a. Privity
b. Comprehensive Environmental Response, Compensation, and Liability Act
c. Blue sky law
d. Privacy Act of 1974

Chapter 12. Work study

1. _____, widely known as F. W. Taylor, was an American mechanical engineer who sought to improve industrial efficiency. He is regarded as the father of scientific management, and was one of the first management consultants.

Taylor was one of the intellectual leaders of the Efficiency Movement and his ideas, broadly conceived, were highly influential in the Progressive Era.

   a. Jonah Jacob Goldberg
   b. Douglas N. Daft
   c. Geoffrey Colvin
   d. Frederick Winslow Taylor

2. _____ is a strategic planning method used to evaluate the Strengths, Weaknesses, Opportunities, and Threats involved in a project or in a business venture. It involves specifying the objective of the business venture or project and identifying the internal and external factors that are favorable and unfavorable to achieving that objective. The technique is credited to Albert Humphrey, who led a convention at Stanford University in the 1960s and 1970s using data from Fortune 500 companies.
   a. Corporate image
   b. SWOT analysis
   c. Marketing
   d. Market share

3. In economics and sociology, an _____ is any factor (financial or non-financial) that enables or motivates a particular course of action, or counts as a reason for preferring one choice to the alternatives. It is an expectation that encourages people to behave in a certain way. Since human beings are purposeful creatures, the study of _____ structures is central to the study of all economic activity (both in terms of individual decision-making and in terms of co-operation and competition within a larger institutional structure.)
   a. AAAI
   b. A4e
   c. A Stake in the Outcome
   d. Incentive

4. A time and motion study (or time-motion study) is a business efficiency technique combining the _____ work of Frederick Winslow Taylor with the Motion Study work of Frank and Lillian Gilbreth (not to be confused with their son, best known through the biographical 1950 film and book Cheaper by the Dozen.) It is a major part of scientific management (Taylorism.)

A time and motion study would be used to reduce the number of motions in performing a task in order to increase productivity.

a. 33 Strategies of War
b. 1990 Clean Air Act
c. 28-hour day
d. Time study

5. The _____ system was developed by AMD in the mid-1990s as a method of comparing their x86 processors to those of rival Intel.

The first use of the _____ system was in 1996, when AMD used it to assert that their AMD 5x86 processor was as fast as a Pentium running at 75 MHz. The designation 'P75' was added to the chip to denote this.

a. 1990 Clean Air Act
b. 28-hour day
c. 33 Strategies of War
d. Performance rating

6. The doctrine of _____ in contract law provides that a contract cannot confer rights or impose obligations arising under it on any person or agent except the parties to it.

The premise is that only parties to contracts should be able to sue to enforce their rights or claim damages as such. However, the doctrine has proven problematic due to its implications upon contracts made for the benefit of third parties who are unable to enforce the obligations of the contracting parties.

a. Blue sky law
b. Privacy Act of 1974
c. Comprehensive Environmental Response, Compensation, and Liability Act
d. Privity

Chapter 13. Costing and pricing

1. _____ is a business management strategy aimed at embedding awareness of quality in all organizational processes. _____ has been widely used in manufacturing, education, hospitals, call centers, government, and service industries, as well as NASA space and science programs.

As defined by the International Organization for Standardization (ISO):

'_____ is a management approach for an organization, centered on quality, based on the participation of all its members and aiming at long-term success through customer satisfaction, and benefits to all members of the organization and to society.' ISO 8402:1994

One major aim is to reduce variation from every process so that greater consistency of effort is obtained. (Royse, D., Thyer, B., Padgett D., ' Logan T., 2006)

   a. Quality management
   b. 1990 Clean Air Act
   c. 28-hour day
   d. Total quality management

2. In economics, business, retail, and accounting, a _____ is the value of money that has been used up to produce something, and hence is not available for use anymore. In economics, a _____ is an alternative that is given up as a result of a decision. In business, the _____ may be one of acquisition, in which case the amount of money expended to acquire it is counted as _____.
   a. Cost allocation
   b. Fixed costs
   c. Cost overrun
   d. Cost

3. _____ are costs that are not directly accountable to a particular function or product. _____ may be either fixed or variable. _____ include taxes, administration, personnel and security costs, and are also known as overhead.
   a. Indirect costs
   b. Activity-based management
   c. A Stake in the Outcome
   d. A4e

4. Marketing research is a form of business research and is generally divided into two categories: consumer _____ and business-to-business (B2B) _____, which was previously known as industrial marketing research. Consumer marketing research studies the buying habits of individual people while business-to-business marketing research investigates the markets for products sold by one business to another.

Consumer _____ is a form of applied sociology that concentrates on understanding the behaviours, whims and preferences, of consumers in a market-based economy, and aims to understand the effects and comparative success of marketing campaigns.

   a. Questionnaire construction
   b. Mystery shoppers
   c. Questionnaire
   d. Market research

5. The doctrine of _____ in contract law provides that a contract cannot confer rights or impose obligations arising under it on any person or agent except the parties to it.

The premise is that only parties to contracts should be able to sue to enforce their rights or claim damages as such. However, the doctrine has proven problematic due to its implications upon contracts made for the benefit of third parties who are unable to enforce the obligations of the contracting parties.

   a. Blue sky law
   b. Privity
   c. Privacy Act of 1974
   d. Comprehensive Environmental Response, Compensation, and Liability Act

6. _____ or net present worth (NPW) is defined as the total present value (PV) of a time series of cash flows. It is a standard method for using the time value of money to appraise long-term projects. Used for capital budgeting, and widely throughout economics, it measures the excess or shortfall of cash flows, in present value terms, once financing charges are met.
   a. Net present value
   b. Discounted cash flow
   c. Present value
   d. 1990 Clean Air Act

7. _____ is the value on a given date of a future payment or series of future payments, discounted to reflect the time value of money and other factors such as investment risk. _____ calculations are widely used in business and economics to provide a means to compare cash flows at different times on a meaningful 'like to like' basis.

If offered a choice between $100 today or $100 in one year, everyone will choose $100 today.

Chapter 13. Costing and pricing

a. Discounted cash flow
b. 1990 Clean Air Act
c. Net present value
d. Present value

8. In economics, _____ are business expenses that are not dependent on the activities of the business They tend to be time-related, such as salaries or rents being paid per month. This is in contrast to variable costs, which are volume-related (and are paid per quantity.)

In management accounting, _____ are defined as expenses that do not change in proportion to the activity of a business, within the relevant period or scale of production.

a. Transaction cost
b. Cost allocation
c. Fixed costs
d. Cost of quality

9. _____s are expenses that change in proportion to the activity of a business. In other words, _____ is the sum of marginal costs. It can also be considered normal costs.
a. Cost accounting
b. Fixed costs
c. Cost overrun
d. Variable cost

10. _____ generally refers to a list of all planned expenses and revenues. It is a plan for saving and spending. A _____ is an important concept in microeconomics, which uses a _____ line to illustrate the trade-offs between two or more goods.
a. 1990 Clean Air Act
b. 33 Strategies of War
c. Budget
d. 28-hour day

11. _____ is one of the four Ps of the marketing mix. The other three aspects are product, promotion, and place. It is also a key variable in microeconomic price allocation theory.

a. Penetration pricing
b. Transfer pricing
c. Price floor
d. Pricing

12. _____, or Value optimized pricing is a business strategy. It sets selling prices on the perceived value to the customer, rather than on the actual cost of the product, the market price, competitors prices, or the historical price.

The goal of value-based pricing is to align price with value delivered.

a. Supervisory board
b. Chief legal officer
c. Centralization
d. Value based pricing

13. In economics, _____ is a rise in the general level of prices of goods and services in an economy over a period of time. When the general price level rises, each unit of the functional currency buys fewer goods and services; consequently, _____ is a decline in the real value of money--a loss of purchasing power in the internal medium of exchange which is also the monetary unit of account in an economy. A chief measure of general price-level _____ is the general _____ rate, which is the percentage change in a general price index (normally the Consumer Price Index) over time.

a. A Stake in the Outcome
b. Economy
c. A4e
d. Inflation

14. In economics, _____ is the desire to own something and the ability to pay for it. The term _____ signifies the ability or the willingness to buy a particular commodity at a given point of time.

a. 28-hour day
b. 1990 Clean Air Act
c. Demand
d. 33 Strategies of War

15. _____ is an economic model based on price, utility and quantity in a market. It concludes that in a competitive market, price will function to equalize the quantity demanded by consumers, and the quantity supplied by producers, resulting in an economic equilibrium of price and quantity. Similarly, an increase in the number of workers tends to result in lower wages and vice-versa.

a. Supply and demand
b. 28-hour day
c. 33 Strategies of War
d. 1990 Clean Air Act

Chapter 14. Measuring financial performance

1. The doctrine of _____ in contract law provides that a contract cannot confer rights or impose obligations arising under it on any person or agent except the parties to it.

The premise is that only parties to contracts should be able to sue to enforce their rights or claim damages as such. However, the doctrine has proven problematic due to its implications upon contracts made for the benefit of third parties who are unable to enforce the obligations of the contracting parties.

   a. Privacy Act of 1974
   b. Privity
   c. Blue sky law
   d. Comprehensive Environmental Response, Compensation, and Liability Act

2. A _____ also known as a sole trader, or simply proprietorship is a type of business entity which there is only one owner and he has the final word taking all desicions by himself. All debts of the business are debts of the owner and must pay from his personal possessions. This means that the owner has unlimited liabilty.

   a. Business rule
   b. Golden hello
   c. Foreign ownership
   d. Sole proprietorship

3. A _____ is a type of business entity in which partners (owners) share with each other the profits or losses of the business. _____s are often favored over corporations for taxation purposes, as the _____ structure does not generally incur a tax on profits before it is distributed to the partners (i.e. there is no dividend tax levied.) However, depending on the _____ structure and the jurisdiction in which it operates, owners of a _____ may be exposed to greater personal liability than they would as shareholders of a corporation.

   a. Federal Employers Liability Act
   b. Due process
   c. Mediation
   d. Partnership

4. _____ is a cornerstone of accrual accounting together with the revenue recognition principle. They both determine the accounting period, in which revenues and expenses are recognized. According to the principle, expenses are recognized when obligations are (1) incurred (usually when goods are transferred or services rendered, e.g. sold), and (2) offset against recognized revenues, which were generated from those expenses (related on the cause-and-effect basis), no matter when cash is paid out.

   a. Treasury stock
   b. Matching principle
   c. Depreciation
   d. Generally accepted accounting principles

Chapter 14. Measuring financial performance

5. _____ generally refers to a list of all planned expenses and revenues. It is a plan for saving and spending. A _____ is an important concept in microeconomics, which uses a _____ line to illustrate the trade-offs between two or more goods.
   a. 33 Strategies of War
   b. 28-hour day
   c. 1990 Clean Air Act
   d. Budget

6. In financial accounting, a _____ or statement of financial position is a summary of a person's or organization's balances. Assets, liabilities and ownership equity are listed as of a specific date, such as the end of its financial year. A _____ is often described as a snapshot of a company's financial condition.
   a. 1990 Clean Air Act
   b. 28-hour day
   c. Balance sheet
   d. 33 Strategies of War

7. _____ is a work methodology based on the parallelization of tasks (ie. concurrently.) It refers to an approach used in product development in which functions of design engineering, manufacturing engineering and other functions are integrated to reduce the elapsed time required to bring a new product to the market.
   a. Critical Chain Project Management
   b. Project management
   c. Work package
   d. Concurrent engineering

8. _____ or net present worth (NPW) is defined as the total present value (PV) of a time series of cash flows. It is a standard method for using the time value of money to appraise long-term projects. Used for capital budgeting, and widely throughout economics, it measures the excess or shortfall of cash flows, in present value terms, once financing charges are met.
   a. Present value
   b. 1990 Clean Air Act
   c. Discounted cash flow
   d. Net present value

9. _____ is the value on a given date of a future payment or series of future payments, discounted to reflect the time value of money and other factors such as investment risk. _____ calculations are widely used in business and economics to provide a means to compare cash flows at different times on a meaningful 'like to like' basis.

If offered a choice between $100 today or $100 in one year, everyone will choose $100 today.

a. Present value
b. Net present value
c. 1990 Clean Air Act
d. Discounted cash flow

10. In business and accounting, _____s are everything of value that is owned by a person or company. Any property or object of value that one possesses, usually considered as applicable to the payment of one's debts is considered an _____. Simplistically stated, _____s are things of value that can be readily converted into cash.

a. AAAI
b. A4e
c. A Stake in the Outcome
d. Asset

11. _____s (CAPEX or capex) are expenditures creating future benefits. A _____ is incurred when a business spends money either to buy fixed assets or to add to the value of an existing fixed asset with a useful life that extends beyond the taxable year. Capex are used by a company to acquire or upgrade physical assets such as equipment, property, or industrial buildings.

a. Weighted average cost of capital
b. 1990 Clean Air Act
c. Capital intensive
d. Capital expenditure

12. _____ is a term used in accounting, economics and finance to spread the cost of an asset over the span of several years.

In simple words we can say that _____ is the reduction in the value of an asset due to usage, passage of time, wear and tear, technological outdating or obsolescence, depletion, inadequacy, rot, rust, decay or other such factors.

In accounting, _____ is a term used to describe any method of attributing the historical or purchase cost of an asset across its useful life, roughly corresponding to normal wear and tear.

a. Net profit
b. Matching principle
c. Treasury stock
d. Depreciation

Chapter 14. Measuring financial performance

13. In finance, the _____ approach describes a method of valuing a project, company, or asset using the concepts of the time value of money. All future cash flows are estimated and discounted to give their present values. The discount rate used is generally the appropriate WACC, that reflects the risk of the cashflows.
    a. Present value
    b. Net present value
    c. 1990 Clean Air Act
    d. Discounted cash flow

14. _____ plant, and equipment, is a term used in accountancy for assets and property which cannot easily be converted into cash. This can be compared with current assets such as cash or bank accounts, which are described as liquid assets. In most cases, only tangible assets are referred to as fixed.
    a. 28-hour day
    b. 1990 Clean Air Act
    c. 33 Strategies of War
    d. Fixed asset

15. In accounting, a _____ is an asset on the balance sheet which is expected to be sold or otherwise used up in the near future, usually within one year, or one business cycle - whichever is longer. Typical _____s include cash, cash equivalents, accounts receivable, inventory, the portion of prepaid accounts which will be used within a year, and short-term investments.

    On the balance sheet, assets will typically be classified into _____s and long-term assets.

    a. Treasury stock
    b. Current asset
    c. Matching principle
    d. Net income

16. _____ is a financial metric which represents operating liquidity available to a business. Along with fixed assets such as plant and equipment, _____ is considered a part of operating capital. It is calculated as current assets minus current liabilities.
    a. Working capital
    b. 1990 Clean Air Act
    c. 33 Strategies of War
    d. 28-hour day

Chapter 14. Measuring financial performance

17. _____ is a statistical technique in decision making that is used for selection of a limited number of tasks that produce significant overall effect. It uses the Pareto principle - the idea that by doing 20% of work you can generate 80% of the advantage of doing the entire job. Or in terms of quality improvement, a large majority of problems (80%) are produced by a few key causes (20%.)
   a. Pareto analysis
   b. Polychoric correlation
   c. Probability matching
   d. Goodness of fit

18. In finance, a _____ or accounting ratio is a ratio of two selected numerical values taken from an enterprise's financial statements. There are many standard ratios used to try to evaluate the overall financial condition of a corporation or other organization. _____s may be used by managers within a firm, by current and potential shareholders (owners) of a firm, and by a firm's creditors.
   a. Rate of return
   b. Return on equity
   c. Return on sales
   d. Financial ratio

19. In accounting, _____ or sales profit is the difference between revenue and the cost of making a product or providing a service, before deducting overhead, payroll, taxation, and interest payments. Note that this is different from operating profit (earnings before interest and taxes.)

Net sales are calculated:

   Net sales = Sales - Sales returns and allowances.

   a. Gross profit margin
   b. Gross profit
   c. Capital budgeting
   d. Cash flow

20. _____ is a financial ratio used to assess the profitability of a firm's core activities, excluding fixed costs.

The general calculation is:

$$\boxed{}$$

The _____ is related to the net profit margin, which assesses the profitability of an organization after including fixed costs.

Chapter 14. Measuring financial performance

_____ indicates the relationship between net sales revenue and the cost of goods sold.

a. Capital structure
b. Shareholder value
c. Sweat equity
d. Gross profit margin

21. The _____ is a financial term defined as a company's operating expenses as a percentage of revenue. This financial ratio is most commonly used for industries such as railroads which require a large percentage of revenues to maintain operations. In railroading, an _____ of 80 or lower is considered desirable.

a. A4e
b. A Stake in the Outcome
c. AAAI
d. Operating ratio

22. _____, net margin, net _____ or net profit ratio all refer to a measure of profitability. It is calculated by finding the net profit as a percentage of the revenue.

$$\text{Net profit margin} = \frac{\text{Net profit (after taxes)}}{\text{Revenue}} \times 100\%$$

The _____ is mostly used for internal comparison.

a. 1990 Clean Air Act
b. Net profit margin
c. Profit margin
d. Profit maximization

23. _____ is a financial ratio that measures the efficiency of a company's use of its assets in generating sales revenue or sales income to the company.

$$Asset\ Turnover = \frac{Sales}{Average\ Total\ Assets}$$

- 'Sales' is the value of 'Net Sales' or 'Sales' from the company's income statement
- 'Average Total Assets' is the value of 'Total assets' from the company's balance sheet in the beginning and the end of the fiscal period divided by 2.

a. Inventory turnover
b. A4e
c. A Stake in the Outcome
d. Asset turnover

24. In a human resources context, _____ or labor _____ is the rate at which an employer gains and loses employees. Simple ways to describe it are 'how long employees tend to stay' or 'the rate of traffic through the revolving door.' _____ is measured for individual companies and for their industry as a whole. If an employer is said to have a high _____ relative to its competitors, it means that employees of that company have a shorter average tenure than those of other companies in the same industry.

a. Ten year occupational employment projection
b. Continuous
c. Career portfolios
d. Turnover

25. The _____ is a financial ratio that measures whether or not a firm has enough resources to pay its debts over the next 12 months. It compares a firm's current assets to its current liabilities. It is expressed as follows:

$$Current\ ratio = \frac{Current\ Assets}{Current\ Liabilities}$$

For example, if WXY Company's current assets are $50,000,000 and its current liabilities are $40,000,000, then its _____ would be $50,000,000 divided by $40,000,000, which equals 1.25.

a. Times interest earned
b. Current ratio
c. Return on assets
d. Financial ratio

Chapter 14. Measuring financial performance

26. Market _____ is a business, economics or investment term that refers to an asset's ability to be easily converted through an act of buying or selling without causing a significant movement in the price and with minimum loss of value. Money, or cash on hand, is the most liquid asset. An act of exchange of a less liquid asset with a more liquid asset is called liquidation.
   a. 28-hour day
   b. 33 Strategies of War
   c. 1990 Clean Air Act
   d. Liquidity

27. In finance, the _____ or quick ratio or liquid ratio measures the ability of a company to use its near cash or quick assets to immediately extinguish or retire its current liabilities. Quick assets include those current assets that presumably can be quickly converted to cash at close to their book values.

Generally, the acid test ratio should be 1:1 or better, however this varies widely by industry.

   a. Inventory turnover
   b. A4e
   c. A Stake in the Outcome
   d. Acid-test

28. In finance, _____ is borrowing money to supplement existing funds for investment in such a way that the potential positive or negative outcome is magnified and/or enhanced. It generally refers to using borrowed funds, or debt, so as to attempt to increase the returns to equity. Deleveraging is the action of reducing borrowings.
   a. Limited liability corporation
   b. Private equity
   c. Limited partners
   d. Gearing

29. An _____ is any party that makes an investment.

The term has taken on a specific meaning in finance to describe the particular types of people and companies that regularly purchase equity or debt securities for financial gain in exchange for funding an expanding company. Less frequently, the term is applied to parties who purchase real estate, currency, commodity derivatives, personal property, or other assets.

a. Investor
b. AAAI
c. A4e
d. A Stake in the Outcome

Chapter 15. Project investment decisions

1. In economics, business, retail, and accounting, a _____ is the value of money that has been used up to produce something, and hence is not available for use anymore. In economics, a _____ is an alternative that is given up as a result of a decision. In business, the _____ may be one of acquisition, in which case the amount of money expended to acquire it is counted as _____.
   a. Cost allocation
   b. Fixed costs
   c. Cost overrun
   d. Cost

2. _____ is the value on a given date of a future payment or series of future payments, discounted to reflect the time value of money and other factors such as investment risk. _____ calculations are widely used in business and economics to provide a means to compare cash flows at different times on a meaningful 'like to like' basis.

   If offered a choice between $100 today or $100 in one year, everyone will choose $100 today.

   a. 1990 Clean Air Act
   b. Discounted cash flow
   c. Present value
   d. Net present value

3. _____ refers to the movement of cash into or out of a business or financial product. It is usually measured during a specified, finite period of time. Measurement of _____ can be used

   - to determine a project's rate of return or value. The time of _____s into and out of projects are used as inputs in financial models such as internal rate of return, and net present value.
   - to determine problems with a business's liquidity. Being profitable does not necessarily mean being liquid. A company can fail because of a shortage of cash, even while profitable.
   - as an alternate measure of a business's profits when it is believed that accrual accounting concepts do not represent economic realities. For example, a company may be notionally profitable but generating little operational cash (as may be the case for a company that barters its products rather than selling for cash.) In such a case, the company may be deriving additional operating cash by issuing shares evaluating default risk, re-investment requirements, etc.

   _____ is a generic term used differently depending on the context. It may be defined by users for their own purposes.

   a. Cash flow
   b. Gross profit
   c. Sweat equity
   d. Gross profit margin

Chapter 15. Project investment decisions

4. A _____ is a type of business entity in which partners (owners) share with each other the profits or losses of the business. _____s are often favored over corporations for taxation purposes, as the _____ structure does not generally incur a tax on profits before it is distributed to the partners (i.e. there is no dividend tax levied.) However, depending on the _____ structure and the jurisdiction in which it operates, owners of a _____ may be exposed to greater personal liability than they would as shareholders of a corporation.

   a. Mediation
   b. Partnership
   c. Federal Employers Liability Act
   d. Due process

5. In business, the term word _____ refers to a number of procurement practices, aimed at finding, evaluating and engaging suppliers of goods and services:

   - Global _____, a procurement strategy aimed at exploiting global efficiencies in production
   - Strategic _____, a component of supply chain management, for improving and re-evaluating purchasing activities
   - _____, the identification of job candidates through proactive recruiting technique
   - Co-_____, a type of auditing service
   - Low-cost country _____, a procurement strategy for acquiring materials from countries with lower labour and production costs in order to cut operating expenses
   - Corporate _____, a supply chain, purchasing/procurement, and inventory function
   - Second-tier _____, a practice of rewarding suppliers for attempting to achieve minority-owned business spending goals of their customer
   - Netsourcing, a practice of utilizing an established group of businesses, individuals, or hardware ' software applications to streamline or initiate procurement practices by tapping in to and working through a third party provider
   - Inverted _____, a price volatility reduction strategy usually conducted by procurement or supply-chain person by which the value of an organization's waste-stream is maximized by actively seeking out the highest price possible from a range of potential buyers exploiting price trends and other market factors
   - Multisourcing, a strategy that treats a given function, such as IT, as a portfolio of activities, some of which should be outsourced and others of which should be performed by internal staff.
   - Crowdsourcing, using an undefined, generally large group of people or community in the form of an open call to perform a task

In journalism, it can also refer to:

   - Journalism _____, the practice of identifying a person or publication that gives information
   - Single _____, the reuse of content in publishing

Chapter 15. Project investment decisions

In computing, it can refer to:

- Open-_____, the act of releasing previously proprietary software under an open source/free software license
- Power _____ equipment, network devices that will provide power in a Power over Ethernet (PoE) setup

a. Continuous
b. Cost Management
c. Reinforcement
d. Sourcing

6. In economics, _____ is a rise in the general level of prices of goods and services in an economy over a period of time. When the general price level rises, each unit of the functional currency buys fewer goods and services; consequently, _____ is a decline in the real value of money--a loss of purchasing power in the internal medium of exchange which is also the monetary unit of account in an economy. A chief measure of general price-level _____ is the general _____ rate, which is the percentage change in a general price index (normally the Consumer Price Index) over time.

a. Inflation
b. A Stake in the Outcome
c. Economy
d. A4e

7. _____ is the study of how the variation (uncertainty) in the output of a mathematical model can be apportioned, qualitatively or quantitatively, to different sources of variation in the input of a model.

In more general terms uncertainty and sensitivity analyses investigate the robustness of a study when the study includes some form of mathematical modelling. While uncertainty analysis studies the overall uncertainty in the conclusions of the study, _____ tries to identify what source of uncertainty weights more on the study's conclusions.

a. No-bid contract
b. Foreign ownership
c. Sensitivity analysis
d. Policies and procedures

Chapter 16. Maintenance management

1. In economics, business, retail, and accounting, a _____ is the value of money that has been used up to produce something, and hence is not available for use anymore. In economics, a _____ is an alternative that is given up as a result of a decision. In business, the _____ may be one of acquisition, in which case the amount of money expended to acquire it is counted as _____.
   a. Fixed costs
   b. Cost allocation
   c. Cost overrun
   d. Cost

2. _____ is an inventory strategy that strives to improve the return on investment of a business by reducing in-process inventory and its associated carrying costs. To meet _____ objectives, the process relies on signals between different points in the process. This means the process is often driven by a series of signals, or Kanban, which tell production when to make the next part. Kanban are usually 'tickets' but can be simple visual signals, such as the presence or absence of a part on a shelf. Implemented correctly, _____ can dramatically improve a manufacturing organization's return on investment, quality, and efficiency.
   a. 1990 Clean Air Act
   b. 33 Strategies of War
   c. Just-in-time
   d. 28-hour day

3. _____ or lean production, which is often known simply as 'Lean', is a production practice that considers the expenditure of resources for any goal other than the creation of value for the end customer to be wasteful, and thus a target for elimination. Working from the perspective of the customer who consumes a product or service, 'value' is defined as any action or process that a customer would be willing to pay for. Basically, lean is centered around creating more value with less work.
   a. Theory of constraints
   b. Production line
   c. Six Sigma
   d. Lean manufacturing

4. _____ is one of the managerial functions like planning, organizing, staffing and directing. It is an important function because it helps to check the errors and to take the corrective action so that deviation from standards are minimized and stated goals of the organization are achieved in desired manner. According to modern concepts, _____ is a foreseeing action whereas earlier concept of _____ was used only when errors were detected. _____ in management means setting standards, measuring actual performance and taking corrective action.
   a. Schedule of reinforcement
   b. Decision tree pruning
   c. Control
   d. Turnover

Chapter 16. Maintenance management

5. The doctrine of _____ in contract law provides that a contract cannot confer rights or impose obligations arising under it on any person or agent except the parties to it.

The premise is that only parties to contracts should be able to sue to enforce their rights or claim damages as such. However, the doctrine has proven problematic due to its implications upon contracts made for the benefit of third parties who are unable to enforce the obligations of the contracting parties.

a. Blue sky law
b. Privacy Act of 1974
c. Comprehensive Environmental Response, Compensation, and Liability Act
d. Privity

6. _____ is the frequency with which an engineered system or component fails, expressed for example in failures per hour. It is often denoted by the Greek letter >λ and is important in reliability theory.

The _____ of a system usually depends on time, with the rate varying over the life cycle of the system.

a. Heteroskedastic
b. Statistics
c. Correlation
d. Failure rate

Chapter 17. Project management

1. The doctrine of _____ in contract law provides that a contract cannot confer rights or impose obligations arising under it on any person or agent except the parties to it.

The premise is that only parties to contracts should be able to sue to enforce their rights or claim damages as such. However, the doctrine has proven problematic due to its implications upon contracts made for the benefit of third parties who are unable to enforce the obligations of the contracting parties.

   a. Privacy Act of 1974
   b. Blue sky law
   c. Comprehensive Environmental Response, Compensation, and Liability Act
   d. Privity

2. _____ refers to the movement of cash into or out of a business or financial product. It is usually measured during a specified, finite period of time. Measurement of _____ can be used

   - to determine a project's rate of return or value. The time of _____s into and out of projects are used as inputs in financial models such as internal rate of return, and net present value.
   - to determine problems with a business's liquidity. Being profitable does not necessarily mean being liquid. A company can fail because of a shortage of cash, even while profitable.
   - as an alternate measure of a business's profits when it is believed that accrual accounting concepts do not represent economic realities. For example, a company may be notionally profitable but generating little operational cash (as may be the case for a company that barters its products rather than selling for cash.) In such a case, the company may be deriving additional operating cash by issuing shares evaluating default risk, re-investment requirements, etc.

_____ is a generic term used differently depending on the context. It may be defined by users for their own purposes.

   a. Sweat equity
   b. Cash flow
   c. Gross profit
   d. Gross profit margin

3. _____ is the discipline of planning, organizing and managing resources to bring about the successful completion of specific project goals and objectives. It is often closely related to and sometimes conflated with Program management.

A project is a finite endeavor--having specific start and completion dates--undertaken to meet particular goals and objectives, usually to bring about beneficial change or added value.

Chapter 17. Project management

a. Work package
b. Precedence diagram
c. Project management
d. Project engineer

4. The Program (or Project) Evaluation and Review Technique, commonly abbreviated _____, is a model for project management designed to analyze and represent the tasks involved in completing a given project.

_____ is a method to analyze the involved tasks in completing a given project, specially the time needed to complete each task, and identifying the minimum time needed to complete the total project.

_____ was developed primarily to simplify the planning and scheduling of large and complex projects.

a. 33 Strategies of War
b. PERT
c. 28-hour day
d. 1990 Clean Air Act

5. A _____ is a professional in the field of project management. _____s can have the responsibility of the planning, execution, and closing of any project, typically relating to construction industry, architecture, computer networking, telecommunications or software development.

Many other fields in the production, design and service industries also have _____s.

a. Project manager
b. Work package
c. Project management
d. Project engineer

6. _____ is a business management strategy aimed at embedding awareness of quality in all organizational processes. _____ has been widely used in manufacturing, education, hospitals, call centers, government, and service industries, as well as NASA space and science programs.

As defined by the International Organization for Standardization (ISO):

'_____ is a management approach for an organization, centered on quality, based on the participation of all its members and aiming at long-term success through customer satisfaction, and benefits to all members of the organization and to society.' ISO 8402:1994

Chapter 17. Project management

One major aim is to reduce variation from every process so that greater consistency of effort is obtained. (Royse, D., Thyer, B., Padgett D., ' Logan T., 2006)

  a. Quality management
  b. 28-hour day
  c. 1990 Clean Air Act
  d. Total quality management

7. _____ is a work methodology based on the parallelization of tasks (ie. concurrently.) It refers to an approach used in product development in which functions of design engineering, manufacturing engineering and other functions are integrated to reduce the elapsed time required to bring a new product to the market.
  a. Work package
  b. Project management
  c. Critical Chain Project Management
  d. Concurrent engineering

8. In economics, business, retail, and accounting, a _____ is the value of money that has been used up to produce something, and hence is not available for use anymore. In economics, a _____ is an alternative that is given up as a result of a decision. In business, the _____ may be one of acquisition, in which case the amount of money expended to acquire it is counted as _____.
  a. Fixed costs
  b. Cost allocation
  c. Cost overrun
  d. Cost

9. In statistics and image processing, to smooth a data set is to create an approximating function that attempts to capture important patterns in the data, while leaving out noise or other fine-scale structures/rapid phenomena. Many different algorithms are used in _____. One of the most common algorithms is the 'moving average', often used to try to capture important trends in repeated statistical surveys.
  a. Smoothing
  b. 28-hour day
  c. 1990 Clean Air Act
  d. 33 Strategies of War

10. _____ is the process whereby an organization establishes the parameters within which programs, investments, and acquisitions are reaching the desired results. Performance Reference Model of the Federal Enterprise Architecture, 2005.

Chapter 17. Project management

This process of measuring performance often requires the use of statistical evidence to determine progress toward specific defined organizational objectives.

There are many types of measurements.

a. Crisis management
b. Workflow
c. CIFMS
d. Performance measurement

11. _____ generally refers to a list of all planned expenses and revenues. It is a plan for saving and spending. A _____ is an important concept in microeconomics, which uses a _____ line to illustrate the trade-offs between two or more goods.

a. 33 Strategies of War
b. 28-hour day
c. 1990 Clean Air Act
d. Budget

12.

_____ is a systematic method to improve the 'value' of goods or products and services by using an examination of function. Value, as defined, is the ratio of function to cost. Value can therefore be increased by either improving the function or reducing the cost.

a. Capacity planning
b. Cellular manufacturing
c. Master production schedule
d. Value engineering

13. _____ is one of the managerial functions like planning, organizing, staffing and directing. It is an important function because it helps to check the errors and to take the corrective action so that deviation from standards are minimized and stated goals of the organization are achieved in desired manner. According to modern concepts, _____ is a foreseeing action whereas earlier concept of _____ was used only when errors were detected. _____ in management means setting standards, measuring actual performance and taking corrective action.

Chapter 17. Project management

a. Turnover
b. Decision tree pruning
c. Schedule of reinforcement
d. Control

14. A _____ is a research instrument consisting of a series of questions and other prompts for the purpose of gathering information from respondents. Although they are often designed for statistical analysis of the responses, this is not always the case. The _____ was invented by Sir Francis Galton.
    a. Mystery shoppers
    b. Structured interview
    c. Questionnaire construction
    d. Questionnaire

15. In economics, _____ is a rise in the general level of prices of goods and services in an economy over a period of time. When the general price level rises, each unit of the functional currency buys fewer goods and services; consequently, _____ is a decline in the real value of money--a loss of purchasing power in the internal medium of exchange which is also the monetary unit of account in an economy. A chief measure of general price-level _____ is the general _____ rate, which is the percentage change in a general price index (normally the Consumer Price Index) over time.
    a. Economy
    b. A Stake in the Outcome
    c. A4e
    d. Inflation

16. _____ refers either to the study and practice of the managerial and technological aspects of the construction industry (including construction, construction science, _____, and construction technology) or to a business model where one party to a construction contract serves as a construction consultant providing both design and construction advice.

The _____ Association of America says the 120 most common responsibilities of a Construction Manager fall into the following 7 categories: Project Management Planning, Cost Management, Time Management, Quality Management, Contract Administration, Safety Management, and _____ Professional Practice which includes specific activities like defining the responsibilities and management structure of the project management team, organizing and leading by implementing project controls, defining roles and responsibilities and developing communication protocols, and identifying elements of project design and construction likely to give rise to disputes and claims.

Chapter 17. Project management

a. Construction management
b. 33 Strategies of War
c. 1990 Clean Air Act
d. 28-hour day

17. _____ is the management of the flow of goods, information and other resources, including energy and people, between the point of origin and the point of consumption in order to meet the requirements of consumers (frequently, and originally, military organizations.) _____ involves the integration of information, transportation, inventory, warehousing, material-handling, and packaging, and occasionally security. _____ is a channel of the supply chain which adds the value of time and place utility.

a. Logistics
b. 28-hour day
c. Third-party logistics
d. 1990 Clean Air Act

18. _____ or net present worth (NPW) is defined as the total present value (PV) of a time series of cash flows. It is a standard method for using the time value of money to appraise long-term projects. Used for capital budgeting, and widely throughout economics, it measures the excess or shortfall of cash flows, in present value terms, once financing charges are met.

a. Present value
b. Discounted cash flow
c. Net present value
d. 1990 Clean Air Act

19. _____ is the value on a given date of a future payment or series of future payments, discounted to reflect the time value of money and other factors such as investment risk. _____ calculations are widely used in business and economics to provide a means to compare cash flows at different times on a meaningful 'like to like' basis.

If offered a choice between $100 today or $100 in one year, everyone will choose $100 today.

a. 1990 Clean Air Act
b. Discounted cash flow
c. Net present value
d. Present value

Chapter 18. Networks for projects

1. _____ is a work methodology based on the parallelization of tasks (ie. concurrently.) It refers to an approach used in product development in which functions of design engineering, manufacturing engineering and other functions are integrated to reduce the elapsed time required to bring a new product to the market.
   a. Project management
   b. Critical Chain Project Management
   c. Work package
   d. Concurrent engineering

2. The Program (or Project) Evaluation and Review Technique, commonly abbreviated _____, is a model for project management designed to analyze and represent the tasks involved in completing a given project.

   _____ is a method to analyze the involved tasks in completing a given project, specially the time needed to complete each task, and identifying the minimum time needed to complete the total project.

   _____ was developed primarily to simplify the planning and scheduling of large and complex projects.

   a. 33 Strategies of War
   b. 1990 Clean Air Act
   c. 28-hour day
   d. PERT

Chapter 19. Project management — managing construction procurement   53

1. _____ refers either to the study and practice of the managerial and technological aspects of the construction industry (including construction, construction science, _____, and construction technology) or to a business model where one party to a construction contract serves as a construction consultant providing both design and construction advice.

The _____ Association of America says the 120 most common responsibilities of a Construction Manager fall into the following 7 categories: Project Management Planning, Cost Management, Time Management, Quality Management, Contract Administration, Safety Management, and _____ Professional Practice which includes specific activities like defining the responsibilities and management structure of the project management team, organizing and leading by implementing project controls, defining roles and responsibilities and developing communication protocols, and identifying elements of project design and construction likely to give rise to disputes and claims.

 a. 28-hour day
 b. 33 Strategies of War
 c. 1990 Clean Air Act
 d. Construction management

2. _____ or contract administration is the management of contracts made with customers, vendors, partners, or employees. _____ includes negotiating the terms and conditions in contracts and ensuring compliance with the terms and conditions, as well as documenting and agreeing any changes that may arise during its implementation or execution. It can be summarized as the process of systematically and efficiently managing contract creating, execution, and analysis for the purpose of maximizing financial and operational performance and minimizing risk.
 a. World Trade Organization
 b. 1990 Clean Air Act
 c. Network planning and design
 d. Contract management

3. The doctrine of _____ in contract law provides that a contract cannot confer rights or impose obligations arising under it on any person or agent except the parties to it.

The premise is that only parties to contracts should be able to sue to enforce their rights or claim damages as such. However, the doctrine has proven problematic due to its implications upon contracts made for the benefit of third parties who are unable to enforce the obligations of the contracting parties.

 a. Comprehensive Environmental Response, Compensation, and Liability Act
 b. Blue sky law
 c. Privacy Act of 1974
 d. Privity

Chapter 19. Project management — managing construction procurement

4. _____ is the acquisition of goods and/or services at the best possible total cost of ownership, in the right quality and quantity, at the right time, in the right place and from the right source for the direct benefit or use of corporations, individuals generally via a contract. Simple _____ may involve nothing more than repeat purchasing. Complex _____ could involve finding long term partners - or even 'co-destiny' suppliers that might fundamentally commit one organization to another.

a. Golden parachute
b. Procurement
c. Sole proprietorship
d. Psychological pricing

5. _____ refers to the movement of cash into or out of a business or financial product. It is usually measured during a specified, finite period of time. Measurement of _____ can be used

- to determine a project's rate of return or value. The time of _____s into and out of projects are used as inputs in financial models such as internal rate of return, and net present value.
- to determine problems with a business's liquidity. Being profitable does not necessarily mean being liquid. A company can fail because of a shortage of cash, even while profitable.
- as an alternate measure of a business's profits when it is believed that accrual accounting concepts do not represent economic realities. For example, a company may be notionally profitable but generating little operational cash (as may be the case for a company that barters its products rather than selling for cash.) In such a case, the company may be deriving additional operating cash by issuing shares evaluating default risk, re-investment requirements, etc.

_____ is a generic term used differently depending on the context. It may be defined by users for their own purposes.

a. Cash flow
b. Gross profit
c. Sweat equity
d. Gross profit margin

6. _____ is the discipline of planning, organizing and managing resources to bring about the successful completion of specific project goals and objectives. It is often closely related to and sometimes conflated with Program management.

A project is a finite endeavor--having specific start and completion dates--undertaken to meet particular goals and objectives, usually to bring about beneficial change or added value.

a. Project management
b. Precedence diagram
c. Project engineer
d. Work package

Chapter 19. Project management — managing construction procurement

7. In economics, business, retail, and accounting, a _____ is the value of money that has been used up to produce something, and hence is not available for use anymore. In economics, a _____ is an alternative that is given up as a result of a decision. In business, the _____ may be one of acquisition, in which case the amount of money expended to acquire it is counted as _____.
   a. Cost
   b. Fixed costs
   c. Cost overrun
   d. Cost allocation

8. _____, a form of alternative dispute resolution (ADR), is a legal technique for the resolution of disputes outside the courts, wherein the parties to a dispute refer it to one or more persons (the 'arbitrators', 'arbiters' or 'arbitral tribunal'), by whose decision (the 'award') they agree to be bound. It is a settlement technique in which a third party reviews the case and imposes a decision that is legally binding for both sides. Other forms of ADR include mediation (a form of settlement negotiation facilitated by a neutral third party) and non-binding resolution by experts.
   a. AAAI
   b. A Stake in the Outcome
   c. A4e
   d. Arbitration

Chapter 20. Inventory management

1. _____ is the process whereby an organization establishes the parameters within which programs, investments, and acquisitions are reaching the desired results. Performance Reference Model of the Federal Enterprise Architecture, 2005.

This process of measuring performance often requires the use of statistical evidence to determine progress toward specific defined organizational objectives.

There are many types of measurements.

   a. Workflow
   b. CIFMS
   c. Crisis management
   d. Performance measurement

2. _____ is a statistical technique in decision making that is used for selection of a limited number of tasks that produce significant overall effect. It uses the Pareto principle - the idea that by doing 20% of work you can generate 80% of the advantage of doing the entire job. Or in terms of quality improvement, a large majority of problems (80%) are produced by a few key causes (20%.)
   a. Polychoric correlation
   b. Goodness of fit
   c. Probability matching
   d. Pareto analysis

3. _____ is an inventory strategy that strives to improve the return on investment of a business by reducing in-process inventory and its associated carrying costs. To meet _____ objectives, the process relies on signals between different points in the process. This means the process is often driven by a series of signals, or Kanban , which tell production when to make the next part. Kanban are usually 'tickets' but can be simple visual signals, such as the presence or absence of a part on a shelf. Implemented correctly, _____ can dramatically improve a manufacturing organization's return on investment, quality, and efficiency.
   a. 33 Strategies of War
   b. 1990 Clean Air Act
   c. 28-hour day
   d. Just-in-time

4. _____ is a concept related to lean and just-in-time (JIT) production. The Japanese word _____ is a common term meaning 'signboard' or 'billboard'. According to Taiichi Ohno, the man credited with developing JIT, _____ is a means through which JIT is achieved.

a. Trademark
b. Risk management
c. Kanban
d. Succession planning

5. _____ is the management of the flow of goods, information and other resources, including energy and people, between the point of origin and the point of consumption in order to meet the requirements of consumers (frequently, and originally, military organizations.) _____ involves the integration of information, transportation, inventory, warehousing, material-handling, and packaging, and occasionally security. _____ is a channel of the supply chain which adds the value of time and place utility.
   a. 28-hour day
   b. Third-party logistics
   c. 1990 Clean Air Act
   d. Logistics

Chapter 21. Management of the supply system

1. A _____ is the system of organizations, people, technology, activities, information and resources involved in moving a product or service from supplier to customer. _____ activities transform natural resources, raw materials and components into a finished product that is delivered to the end customer. In sophisticated _____ systems, used products may re-enter the _____ at any point where residual value is recyclable.
   a. Packaging
   b. Drop shipping
   c. Wholesalers
   d. Supply chain

2. The doctrine of _____ in contract law provides that a contract cannot confer rights or impose obligations arising under it on any person or agent except the parties to it.

   The premise is that only parties to contracts should be able to sue to enforce their rights or claim damages as such. However, the doctrine has proven problematic due to its implications upon contracts made for the benefit of third parties who are unable to enforce the obligations of the contracting parties.

   a. Privity
   b. Comprehensive Environmental Response, Compensation, and Liability Act
   c. Blue sky law
   d. Privacy Act of 1974

3. A _____ is a type of business entity in which partners (owners) share with each other the profits or losses of the business. _____s are often favored over corporations for taxation purposes, as the _____ structure does not generally incur a tax on profits before it is distributed to the partners (i.e. there is no dividend tax levied.) However, depending on the _____ structure and the jurisdiction in which it operates, owners of a _____ may be exposed to greater personal liability than they would as shareholders of a corporation.
   a. Federal Employers Liability Act
   b. Due process
   c. Mediation
   d. Partnership

Chapter 21. Management of the supply system

4. In business, the term word _____ refers to a number of procurement practices, aimed at finding, evaluating and engaging suppliers of goods and services:

- Global _____, a procurement strategy aimed at exploiting global efficiencies in production
- Strategic _____, a component of supply chain management, for improving and re-evaluating purchasing activities
- _____, the identification of job candidates through proactive recruiting technique
- Co-_____, a type of auditing service
- Low-cost country _____, a procurement strategy for acquiring materials from countries with lower labour and production costs in order to cut operating expenses
- Corporate _____, a supply chain, purchasing/procurement, and inventory function
- Second-tier _____, a practice of rewarding suppliers for attempting to achieve minority-owned business spending goals of their customer
- Netsourcing, a practice of utilizing an established group of businesses, individuals, or hardware ' software applications to streamline or initiate procurement practices by tapping in to and working through a third party provider
- Inverted _____, a price volatility reduction strategy usually conducted by procurement or supply-chain person by which the value of an organization's waste-stream is maximized by actively seeking out the highest price possible from a range of potential buyers exploiting price trends and other market factors
- Multisourcing, a strategy that treats a given function, such as IT, as a portfolio of activities, some of which should be outsourced and others of which should be performed by internal staff.
- Crowdsourcing, using an undefined, generally large group of people or community in the form of an open call to perform a task

In journalism, it can also refer to:

- Journalism _____, the practice of identifying a person or publication that gives information
- Single _____, the reuse of content in publishing

In computing, it can refer to:

- Open-_____, the act of releasing previously proprietary software under an open source/free software license
- Power _____ equipment, network devices that will provide power in a Power over Ethernet (PoE) setup

a. Reinforcement
b. Sourcing
c. Continuous
d. Cost Management

5. _____ is used in finance as a measure of the returns that a company is realising from its capital employed. It is commonly used as a measure for comparing the performance between businesses and for assessing whether a business generates enough returns to pay for its cost of capital.

Chapter 21. Management of the supply system

Net Profit / Capital Employed X 100

_____ compares earnings with capital invested in the company.

a. Financial ratio
b. Return on equity
c. Return on Capital Employed
d. Times interest earned

6. In finance, a _____ or accounting ratio is a ratio of two selected numerical values taken from an enterprise's financial statements. There are many standard ratios used to try to evaluate the overall financial condition of a corporation or other organization. _____s may be used by managers within a firm, by current and potential shareholders (owners) of a firm, and by a firm's creditors.
a. Financial ratio
b. Return on sales
c. Return on equity
d. Rate of return

7. _____ is the management of the flow of goods, information and other resources, including energy and people, between the point of origin and the point of consumption in order to meet the requirements of consumers (frequently, and originally, military organizations.) _____ involves the integration of information, transportation, inventory, warehousing, material-handling, and packaging, and occasionally security. _____ is a channel of the supply chain which adds the value of time and place utility.
a. 1990 Clean Air Act
b. Third-party logistics
c. 28-hour day
d. Logistics

8. A _____ is typically described as a deliberate plan of action to guide decisions and achieve rational outcome(s.) However, the term may also be used to denote what is actually done, even though it is unplanned.

The term may apply to government, private sector organizations and groups, and individuals.

a. 33 Strategies of War
b. 28-hour day
c. 1990 Clean Air Act
d. Policy

Chapter 21. Management of the supply system

9. _____ is a financial metric which represents operating liquidity available to a business. Along with fixed assets such as plant and equipment, _____ is considered a part of operating capital. It is calculated as current assets minus current liabilities.
   a. 1990 Clean Air Act
   b. Working capital
   c. 28-hour day
   d. 33 Strategies of War

62   *Chapter 22. Marketing*

1. _____ is an integrated communications-based process through which individuals and communities discover that existing and newly-identified needs and wants may be satisfied by the products and services of others.

_____ is defined by the American _____ Association as the activity, set of institutions, and processes for creating, communicating, delivering, and exchanging offerings that have value for customers, clients, partners, and society at large. The term developed from the original meaning which referred literally to going to market, as in shopping, or going to a market to buy or sell goods or services.

   a. Customer relationship management
   b. Market development
   c. Disruptive technology
   d. Marketing

2. _____ is a strategic planning method used to evaluate the Strengths, Weaknesses, Opportunities, and Threats involved in a project or in a business venture. It involves specifying the objective of the business venture or project and identifying the internal and external factors that are favorable and unfavorable to achieving that objective. The technique is credited to Albert Humphrey, who led a convention at Stanford University in the 1960s and 1970s using data from Fortune 500 companies.
   a. Corporate image
   b. SWOT analysis
   c. Marketing
   d. Market share

3. The _____ is generally accepted as the use and specification of the 'four P's' describing the strategic position of a product in the marketplace. One version of the _____ originated in 1948 when James Culliton said that a marketing decision should be a result of something similar to a recipe. This version was used in 1953 when Neil Borden, in his American Marketing Association presidential address, took the recipe idea one step further and coined the term 'marketing-mix'.
   a. Marketing mix
   b. 33 Strategies of War
   c. 1990 Clean Air Act
   d. 28-hour day

4. _____ Management is the succession of strategies used by management as a product goes through its _____. The conditions in which a product is sold changes over time and must be managed as it moves through its succession of stages.

The _____ goes through many phases, involves many professional disciplines, and requires many skills, tools and processes.

Chapter 22. Marketing

a. Golden handshake
b. Job hunting
c. Strategic Alliance
d. Product life cycle

5. A _____ is a group of people or organizations sharing one or more characteristics that cause them to have similar product and/or service needs. A true _____ meets all of the following criteria: it is distinct from other segments (different segments have different needs), it is homogeneous within the segment (exhibits common needs); it responds similarly to a market stimulus, and it can be reached by a market intervention. The term is also used when consumers with identical product and/or service needs are divided up into groups so they can be charged different amounts.
   a. Customer relationship management
   b. Context analysis
   c. SWOT analysis
   d. Market segment

6. The _____ is a concept from business management that was first described and popularized by Michael Porter in his 1985 best-seller, Competitive Advantage: Creating and Sustaining Superior Performance.

A _____ is a chain of activities. Products pass through all activities of the chain in order and at each activity the product gains some value. The chain of activities gives the products more added value than the sum of added values of all activities. It is important not to mix the concept of the _____ with the costs occurring throughout the activities.

   a. Mass marketing
   b. Customer relationship management
   c. Value chain
   d. Market development

7. A _____ is a type of bar chart that illustrates a project schedule. _____s illustrate the start and finish dates of the terminal elements and summary elements of a project. Terminal elements and summary elements comprise the work breakdown structure of the project.
   a. 33 Strategies of War
   b. 28-hour day
   c. 1990 Clean Air Act
   d. Gantt chart

8. The doctrine of _____ in contract law provides that a contract cannot confer rights or impose obligations arising under it on any person or agent except the parties to it.

Chapter 22. Marketing

The premise is that only parties to contracts should be able to sue to enforce their rights or claim damages as such. However, the doctrine has proven problematic due to its implications upon contracts made for the benefit of third parties who are unable to enforce the obligations of the contracting parties.

a. Comprehensive Environmental Response, Compensation, and Liability Act
b. Blue sky law
c. Privacy Act of 1974
d. Privity

9. _____ is a form of marketing developed from direct response marketing campaigns conducted in the 1970s and 1980s which emphasizes customer retention and satisfaction, rather than a dominant focus on point-of-sale transactions.

_____ differs from other forms of marketing in that it recognizes the long term value to the firm of keeping customers, as opposed to direct or 'Intrusion' marketing, which focuses upon acquisition of new clients by targeting majority demographics based upon prospective client lists.

_____ refers to a long-term and mutually beneficial arrangement wherein both the buyer and seller focus on value enhancement with the goal of providing a more satisfying exchange.

a. 1990 Clean Air Act
b. Relationship marketing
c. 28-hour day
d. Guerrilla marketing

10. _____ is the value on a given date of a future payment or series of future payments, discounted to reflect the time value of money and other factors such as investment risk. _____ calculations are widely used in business and economics to provide a means to compare cash flows at different times on a meaningful 'like to like' basis.

If offered a choice between $100 today or $100 in one year, everyone will choose $100 today.

a. Present value
b. 1990 Clean Air Act
c. Net present value
d. Discounted cash flow

11. _____ is one of the four Ps of the marketing mix. The other three aspects are product, promotion, and place. It is also a key variable in microeconomic price allocation theory.

a. Price floor
b. Penetration pricing
c. Pricing
d. Transfer pricing

12. _____, or Value optimized pricing is a business strategy. It sets selling prices on the perceived value to the customer, rather than on the actual cost of the product, the market price, competitors prices, or the historical price.

The goal of value-based pricing is to align price with value delivered.

a. Chief legal officer
b. Supervisory board
c. Value based pricing
d. Centralization

13. _____ is a form of communication that typically attempts to persuade potential customers to purchase or to consume more of a particular brand of product or service. 'While now central to the contemporary global economy and the reproduction of global production networks, it is only quite recently that _____ has been more than a marginal influence on patterns of sales and production. The formation of modern _____ was intimately bound up with the emergence of new forms of monopoly capitalism around the end of the 19th and beginning of the 20th century as one element in corporate strategies to create, organize and where possible control markets, especially for mass produced consumer goods.

a. A4e
b. AAAI
c. A Stake in the Outcome
d. Advertising

14. _____ is an inventory strategy that strives to improve the return on investment of a business by reducing in-process inventory and its associated carrying costs. To meet _____ objectives, the process relies on signals between different points in the process. This means the process is often driven by a series of signals, or Kanban , which tell production when to make the next part. Kanban are usually 'tickets' but can be simple visual signals, such as the presence or absence of a part on a shelf. Implemented correctly, _____ can dramatically improve a manufacturing organization's return on investment, quality, and efficiency.

a. 28-hour day
b. 33 Strategies of War
c. 1990 Clean Air Act
d. Just-in-time

15. Marketing research is a form of business research and is generally divided into two categories: consumer _____ and business-to-business (B2B) _____, which was previously known as industrial marketing research. Consumer marketing research studies the buying habits of individual people while business-to-business marketing research investigates the markets for products sold by one business to another.

Consumer _____ is a form of applied sociology that concentrates on understanding the behaviours, whims and preferences, of consumers in a market-based economy, and aims to understand the effects and comparative success of marketing campaigns.

   a. Mystery shoppers
   b. Market research
   c. Questionnaire
   d. Questionnaire construction

Chapter 23. A case study in starting an SME

1. A _____ is a formal statement of a set of business goals, the reasons why they are believed attainable, and the plan for reaching those goals. It may also contain background information about the organization or team attempting to reach those goals.

The business goals may be defined for for-profit or for non-profit organizations.

   a. Crisis management
   b. Distributed management
   c. Time management
   d. Business plan

2. _____ is a family of standards for quality management systems. _____ is maintained by ISO, the International Organization for Standardization and is administered by accreditation and certification bodies. The rules are updated, the time and changes in the requirements for quality, motivate change.
   a. A Stake in the Outcome
   b. A4e
   c. AAAI
   d. ISO 9000

3. _____ is a strategic planning method used to evaluate the Strengths, Weaknesses, Opportunities, and Threats involved in a project or in a business venture. It involves specifying the objective of the business venture or project and identifying the internal and external factors that are favorable and unfavorable to achieving that objective. The technique is credited to Albert Humphrey, who led a convention at Stanford University in the 1960s and 1970s using data from Fortune 500 companies.
   a. Market share
   b. Marketing
   c. SWOT analysis
   d. Corporate image

4. A _____ is a research instrument consisting of a series of questions and other prompts for the purpose of gathering information from respondents. Although they are often designed for statistical analysis of the responses, this is not always the case. The _____ was invented by Sir Francis Galton.
   a. Structured interview
   b. Mystery shoppers
   c. Questionnaire
   d. Questionnaire construction

5. _____ refers either to the study and practice of the managerial and technological aspects of the construction industry (including construction, construction science, _____, and construction technology) or to a business model where one party to a construction contract serves as a construction consultant providing both design and construction advice.

The _____ Association of America says the 120 most common responsibilities of a Construction Manager fall into the following 7 categories: Project Management Planning, Cost Management, Time Management, Quality Management, Contract Administration, Safety Management, and _____ Professional Practice which includes specific activities like defining the responsibilities and management structure of the project management team, organizing and leading by implementing project controls, defining roles and responsibilities and developing communication protocols, and identifying elements of project design and construction likely to give rise to disputes and claims.

a. 33 Strategies of War
b. Construction management
c. 1990 Clean Air Act
d. 28-hour day

6. In finance, the _____ approach describes a method of valuing a project, company, or asset using the concepts of the time value of money. All future cash flows are estimated and discounted to give their present values. The discount rate used is generally the appropriate WACC, that reflects the risk of the cashflows.
a. Net present value
b. Present value
c. 1990 Clean Air Act
d. Discounted cash flow

ANSWER KEY

Chapter 1
    1. c   2. b   3. a   4. a   5. a   6. a

Chapter 2
    1. d   2. d   3. a   4. c

Chapter 3
    1. d   2. d   3. d

Chapter 4
    1. d   2. d   3. c   4. c   5. d   6. a   7. d   8. d   9. d   10. b

Chapter 5
    1. c   2. d

Chapter 6
    1. d   2. b   3. d   4. a

Chapter 7
    1. d   2. d   3. d   4. b   5. a

Chapter 8
    1. d   2. d   3. c   4. d

Chapter 9
    1. b   2. b   3. a   4. d   5. a   6. a   7. c   8. b   9. d

Chapter 10
    1. d   2. d   3. d   4. d   5. a   6. b   7. d   8. d   9. d   10. c
    11. a   12. b   13. c   14. c   15. d   16. d

Chapter 11
    1. c   2. d   3. d   4. a

Chapter 12
    1. d   2. b   3. d   4. d   5. d   6. d

Chapter 13
    1. d   2. d   3. a   4. d   5. b   6. a   7. d   8. c   9. d   10. c
    11. d   12. d   13. d   14. c   15. a

Chapter 14
    1. b   2. d   3. d   4. b   5. d   6. c   7. d   8. d   9. a   10. d
    11. d   12. d   13. d   14. d   15. b   16. a   17. a   18. d   19. b   20. d
    21. d   22. c   23. d   24. d   25. b   26. d   27. d   28. d   29. a

Chapter 15
1. d   2. c   3. a   4. b   5. d   6. a   7. c

Chapter 16
1. d   2. c   3. d   4. c   5. d   6. d

Chapter 17
1. d   2. b   3. c   4. b   5. a   6. d   7. d   8. d   9. a   10. d
11. d   12. d   13. d   14. d   15. d   16. a   17. a   18. c   19. d

Chapter 18
1. d   2. d

Chapter 19
1. d   2. d   3. d   4. b   5. a   6. a   7. a   8. d

Chapter 20
1. d   2. d   3. d   4. c   5. d

Chapter 21
1. d   2. a   3. d   4. b   5. c   6. a   7. d   8. d   9. b

Chapter 22
1. d   2. b   3. a   4. d   5. d   6. c   7. d   8. d   9. b   10. a
11. c   12. c   13. d   14. d   15. b

Chapter 23
1. d   2. d   3. c   4. c   5. b   6. d

www.ingramcontent.com/pod-product-compliance
Lightning Source LLC
Chambersburg PA
CBHW081850230426
43669CB00018B/2889